THIRD
BOOK OF IMPORTANT
DATES

ILLUSTRATED WITH
PAINTINGS OF PEOPLE
BY ELEANOR GILPATRICK

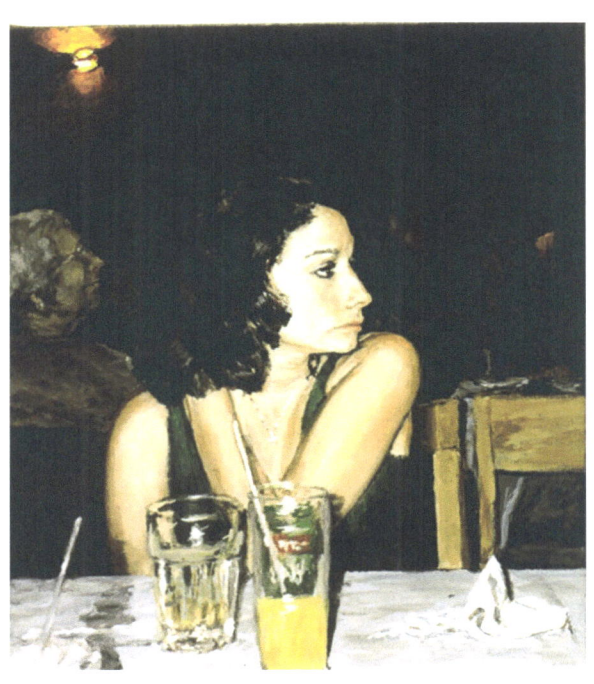

PLEASE NOTE:

The images presented in this book are based on the RGB color system, used when digital images are produced from photographs of paintings. With publication in a book, the CMYK color system is used. Documents that move from a computer screen to a printed page are affected by the fact that there are RGB colors that CMYK printers cannot reproduce. Something that looks good on a monitor may not look the same when printed. To overcome this limitation I have reviewed each printed page in a proof copy, and have made changes to bring the printed pages into as close a representation of the actual paintings as possible.

But the process is not perfect; and a small amount of variance from unit to unit is expected. The color may vary slightly from print run to print run and day to day.

I hope that you will enjoy this book; I encourage you to view the online website where images of the paintings are presented: www.Zibbet.com/Egilpatr

Eleanor Gilpatrick

Cover Image:
On The Beach; 24 x 38 inches

Title Page Image:
J; 16 x 14 inches

Biography Page Image:
In The Deep III; 13 x 35 inches

Book design: Eleanor Gilpatrick

ISBN: 1448654343
EAN-13: 9781448654345.

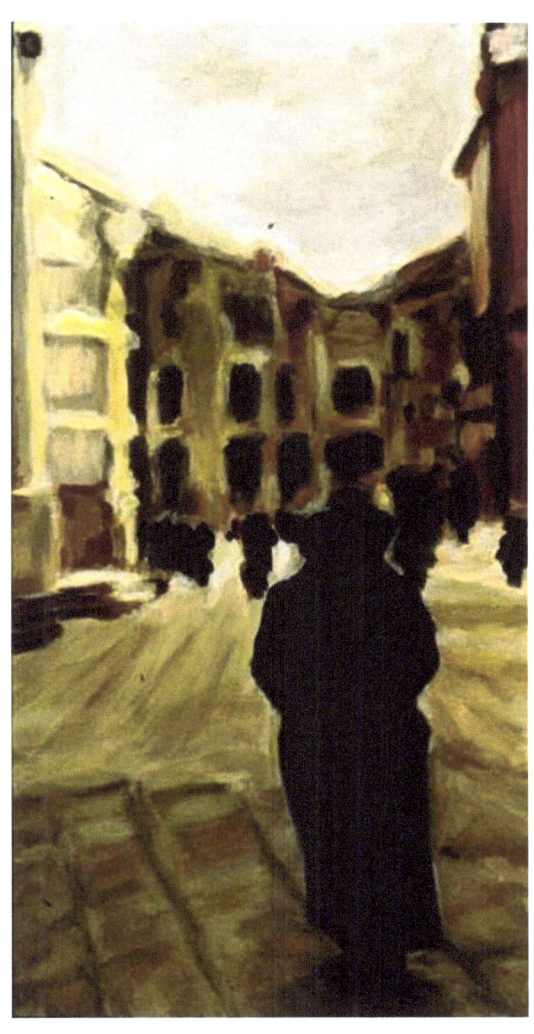

JANUARY

Once is 20 inches high by 10 inches wide; acrylic on canvas. It is based on a photograph I took of my friend when we were in Venice one January. I made it moody and enigmatic. Once we were in Venice and…...………
The original is in a private collection.

JANUARY

1 _____

2 _____

3 _____

4 _____

5 _____

6 _____

7 _____

8 _____

9 _____

10 _____

11 _____

12 _____

13 _____

14 _____

15 _____

16 _____

JANUARY

17 _____

18 _____

19 _____

20 _____

21 _____

22 _____

23 _____

24 _____

25 _____

26 _____

27 _____

28 _____

29 _____

30 _____

31 _____

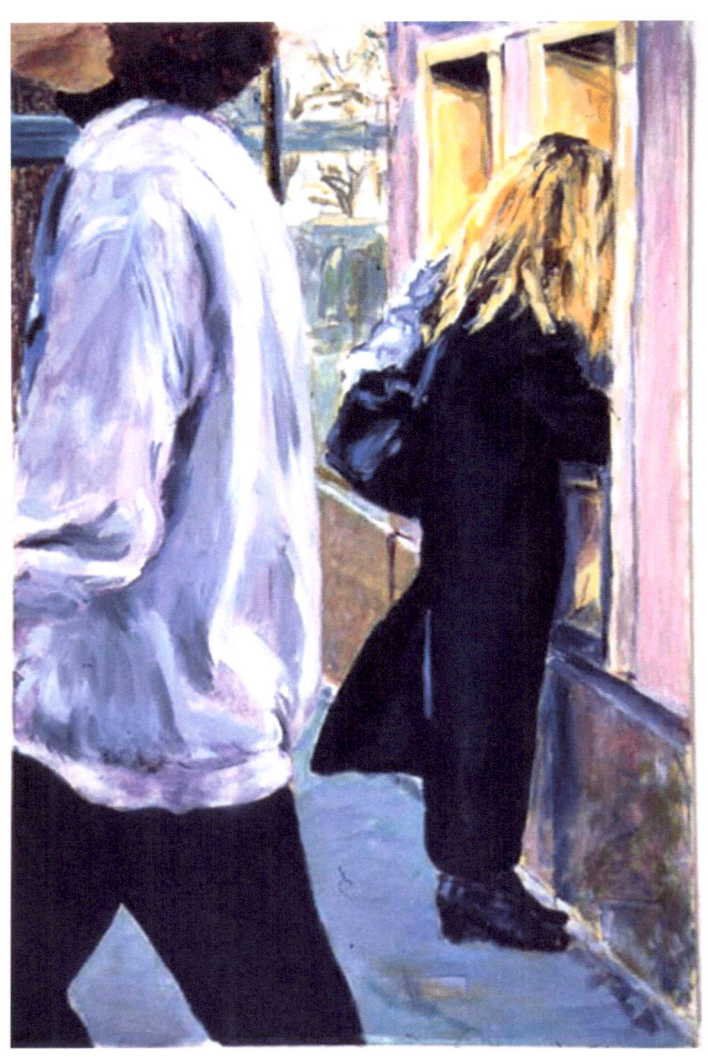

FEBRUARY

The ATM is the third in a 4-part group, January Jog, that follows a jogger around New York City on a winter day. Here she passes a woman at an ATM machine, doing what we all do there. The painting is 28 x 18 inches, alkyd on stretched canvas. The framed dimensions are 30 inches high by 20 inches wide. The painting can be seen at www.Zibbet.com/Egilpatr

FEBRUARY

1 _____

2 _____

3 _____

4 _____

5 _____

6 _____

7 _____

8 _____

9 _____

10 _____

11 _____

12 _____

13 _____

14 _____

15 _____

16 _____

FEBRUARY

17 _____

18 _____

19 _____

20 _____

21 _____

22 _____

23 _____

24 _____

25 _____

26 _____

27 _____

28 _____

29 LEAP YEAR! _____

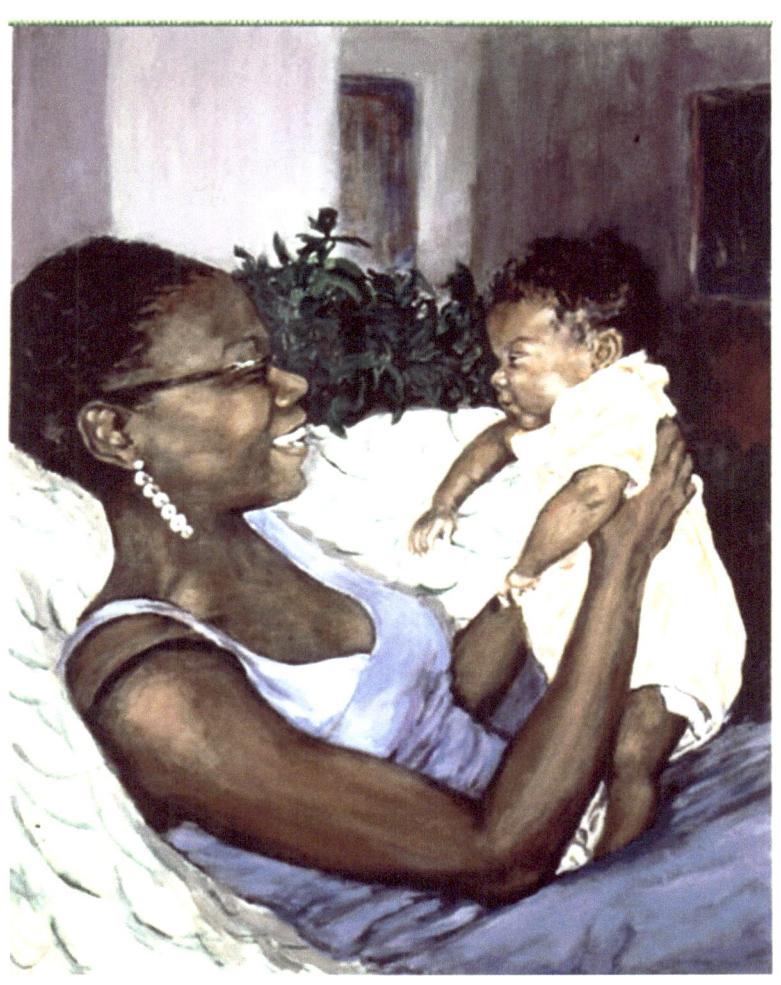

MARCH

Beginning is my love song to a dear friend and her first child; how they looked at each other from the very beginning. This is 28 by 22 inches, acrylic on stretched canvas. The framed dimensions are 30 inches high by 24 inches wide. It is in my friend's private collection.

MARCH

1_____

2_____

3_____

4_____

5_____

6_____

7_____

8_____

9_____

10_____

11_____

12_____

13_____

14_____

15_____

16_____

MARCH

17 _____

18 _____

19 _____

20 _____

21 _____

22 _____

23 _____

24 _____

25 _____

26 _____

27 _____

28 _____

29 _____

30 _____

31 _____

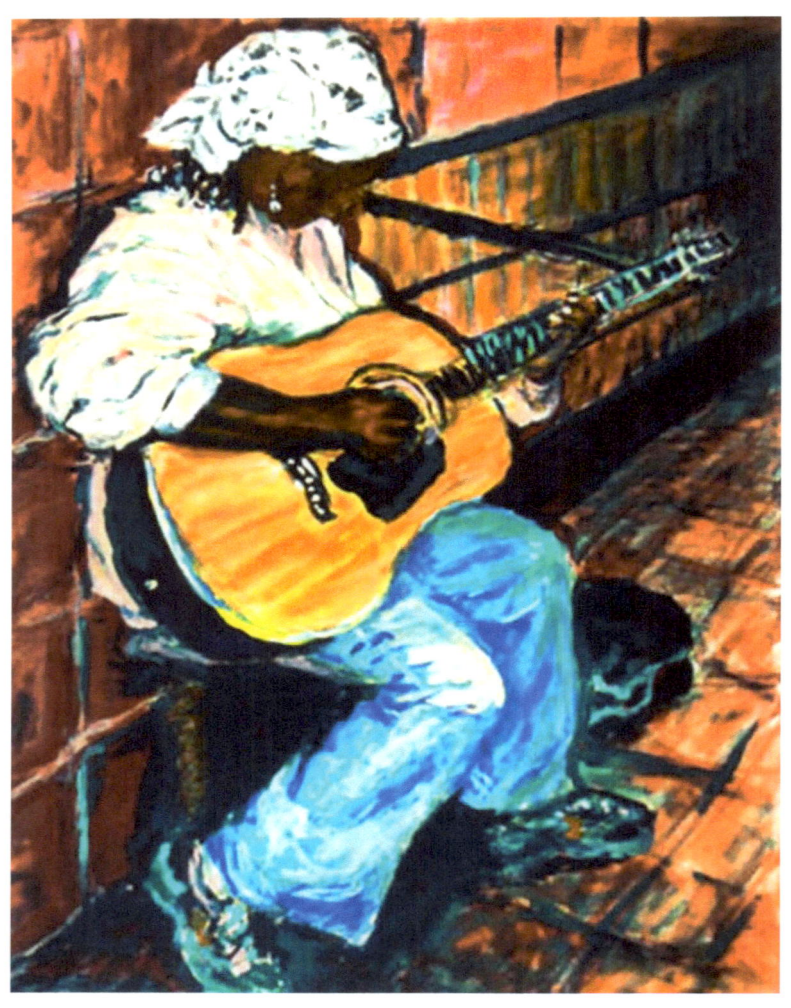

APRIL

Metro Music I portrays a subway musician in New York City, where musicians play in passageways and on platforms, and add some pleasure to the frantic rush. This was the passage between the Number 6 train and the E train at Lexington Ave. The painting is 26 x 20 inches, acrylic on stretched canvas. The framed dimensions are 28 inches high by 22 inches wide. You can see the painting at www.Zibbet.com/Egilpatr

APRIL

1 _____

2 _____

3 _____

4 _____

5 _____

6 _____

7 _____

8 _____

9 _____

10 _____

11 _____

12 _____

13 _____

14 _____

15 _____

16 _____

APRIL

17 _____

18 _____

19 _____

20 _____

21 _____

22 _____

23 _____

24 _____

25 _____

26 _____

27 _____

28 _____

29 _____

30 _____

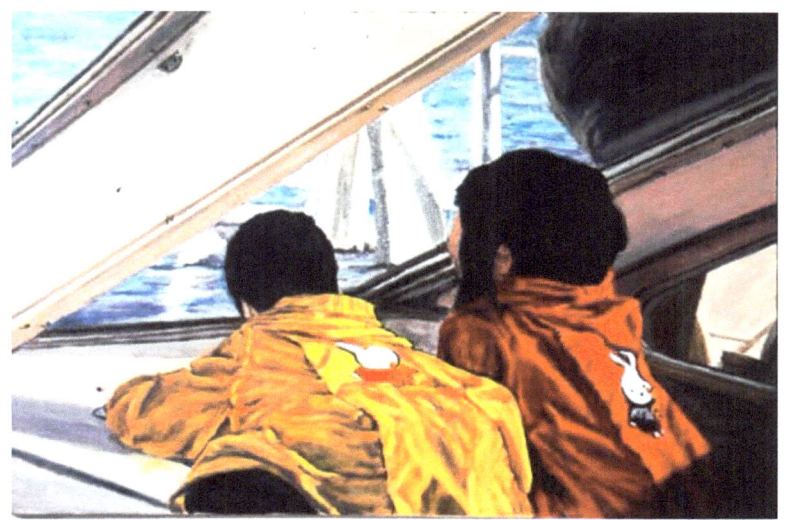

MAY

Express Boat To Balestrand portrays children on a boat headed to Balestrand from Bergen, Norway. The children were enjoying the rush of the water. And I was enjoying the children, who were captivated by the experience.

The painting is 20 x 30 inches, acrylic on stretched canvas, and is framed. The framed dimensions are 22 inches high by 32 inches wide. The original painting can be seen online at www.Zibbet.com/Egilpatr

MAY

1 _____

2 _____

3 _____

4 _____

5 _____

6 _____

7 _____

8 _____

9 _____

10 _____

11 _____

12 _____

13 _____

14 _____

15 _____

16 _____

MAY

17 _____

18 _____

19 _____

20 _____

21 _____

22 _____

23 _____

24 _____

25 _____

26 _____

27 _____

28 _____

29 _____

30 _____

31 _____

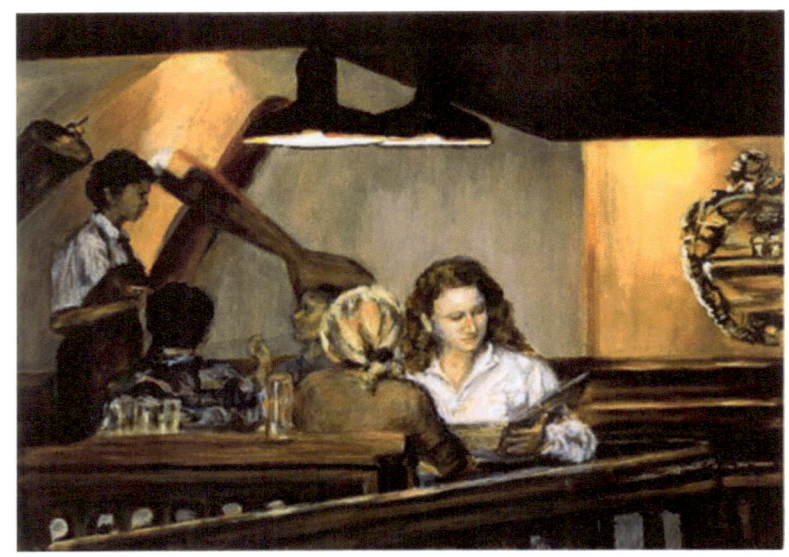

JUNE

El Mussol, Upstairs is set in El Mussol, a restaurant in Barcelona. We had climbed up to the upper level of the restaurant to explore and enjoyed its roomy dimensions. I wanted at once to paint the people and the unusual decor.

The painting is acrylic on stretched canvas on heavy duty stretchers, with painted sides. The original can be seen at www.Zibbet.com/Egilpatr

JUNE

1 _____

2 _____

3 _____

4 _____

5 _____

6 _____

7 _____

8 _____

9 _____

10 _____

11 _____

12 _____

13 _____

14 _____

15 _____

16 _____

JUNE

17 _____

18 _____

19 _____

20 _____

21 _____

22 _____

23 _____

24 _____

25 _____

26 _____

27 _____

28 _____

29 _____

30 _____

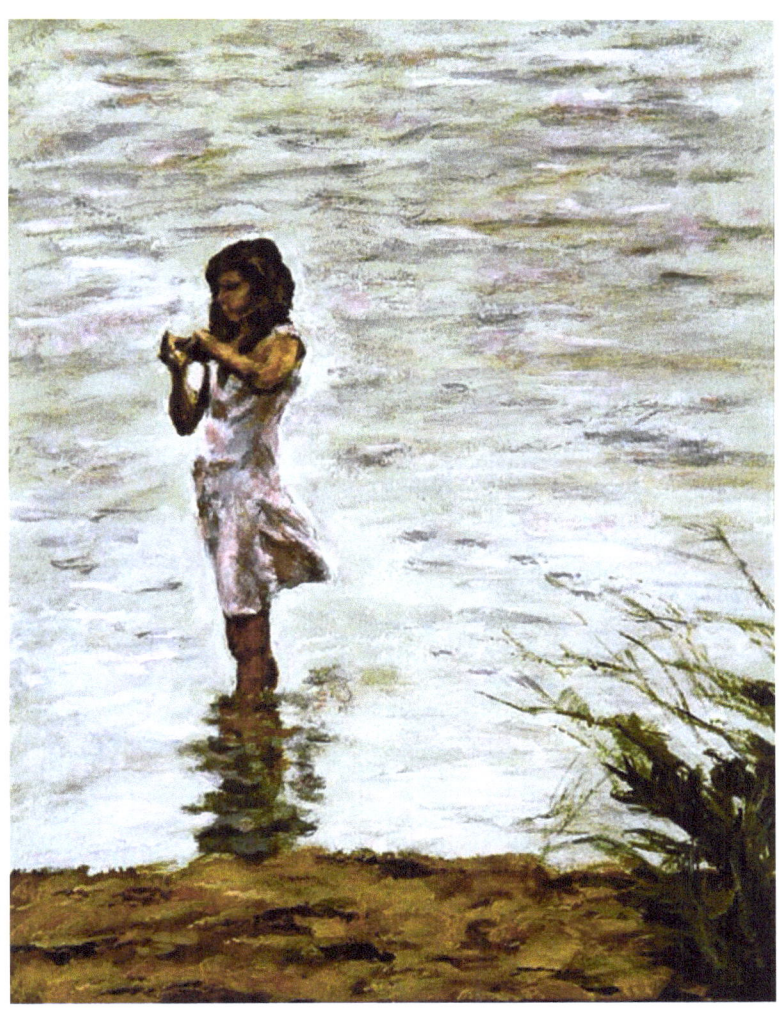

JULY

Misty Light is another painting inspired by East Hampton, NY. Upon revisiting the site of "East Hampton Light" after some stormy years, I found that the area was a bit battered though not much changed. But this water nymph was new. The painting is acrylic on stretched canvas, 16 inches high by 12 inches wide. See the original at www.Zibbet.com/Egilpatr

JULY

1 _____

2 _____

3 _____

4 _____

5 _____

6 _____

7 _____

8 _____

9 _____

10 _____

11 _____

12 _____

13 _____

14 _____

15 _____

16 _____

JULY

17 _____

18 _____

19 _____

20 _____

21 _____

22 _____

23 _____

24 _____

25 _____

26 _____

27 _____

28 _____

29 _____

30 _____

31 _____

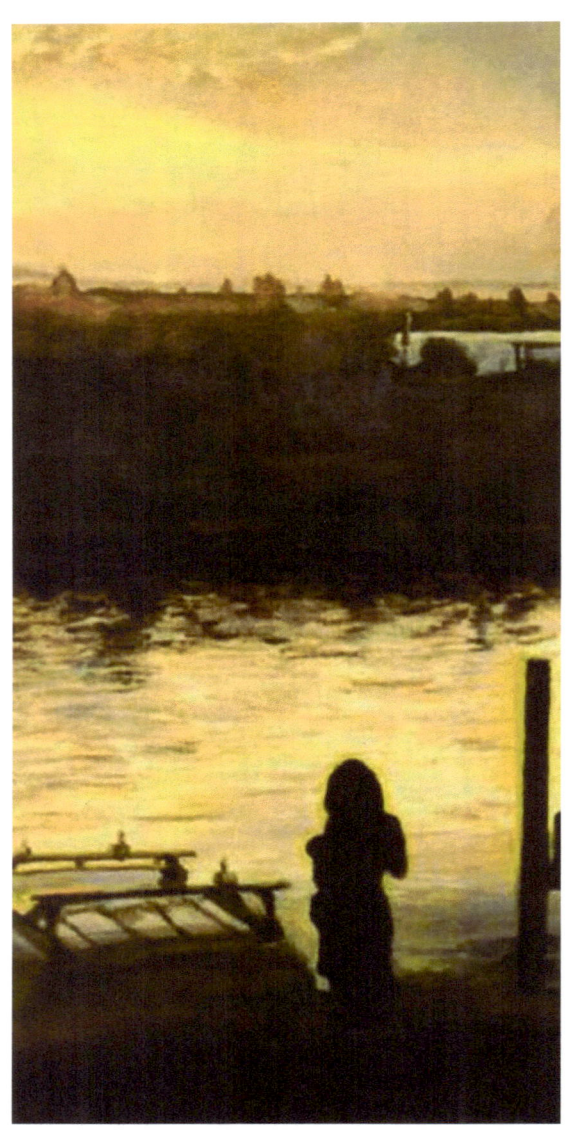

AUGUST

Summer Night I was inspired by an East Hampton, NY, Sunset. We were in a restaurant that looks out over the water at Three Mile Harbor. And I saw the figure of the woman as part of the landscape. The painting is 20 inches high by 10 inches wide, acrylic on stretched canvas, on heavy duty stretchers, with painted sides. It can be seen at www.Zibbet.com/Egilpatr

AUGUST

1 _____

2 _____

3 _____

4 _____

5 _____

6 _____

7 _____

8 _____

9 _____

10 _____

11 _____

12 _____

13 _____

14 _____

15 _____

16 _____

AUGUST

17_____

18_____

19_____

20_____

21_____

22_____

23_____

24_____

25_____

26_____

27_____

28_____

29_____

30_____

31_____

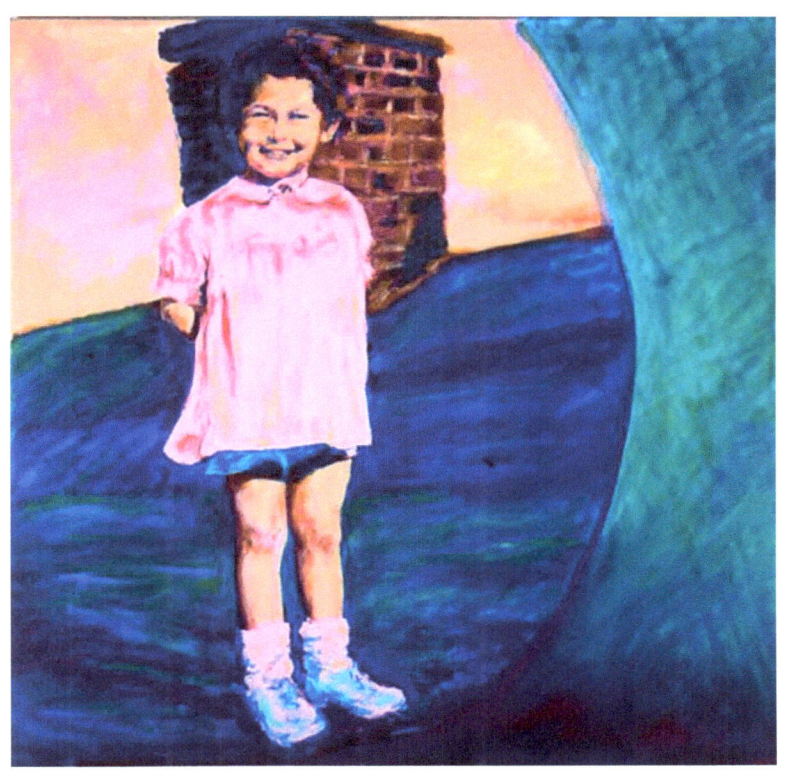

SEPTEMBER

Baby Me is a little girl on a Brooklyn, New York, rooftop in 1936. The picture captures the way children of poor families looked when they were dressed up to be photographed. The photo on which this is based was black and white, and mounted on a small round mirror. The painting is 34 x 34 inches, acrylic on stretched canvas. The framed dimensions are 36 x 36 inches. The original painting is at www.Zibbet.com/Egilpatr

SEPTEMBER

1_____

2_____

3_____

4_____

5_____

6_____

7_____

8_____

9_____

10_____

11_____

12_____

13_____

14_____

15_____

16_____

SEPTEMBER

17 _____

18 _____

19 _____

20 _____

21 _____

22 _____

23 _____

24 _____

25 _____

26 _____

27 _____

28 _____

29 _____

30 _____

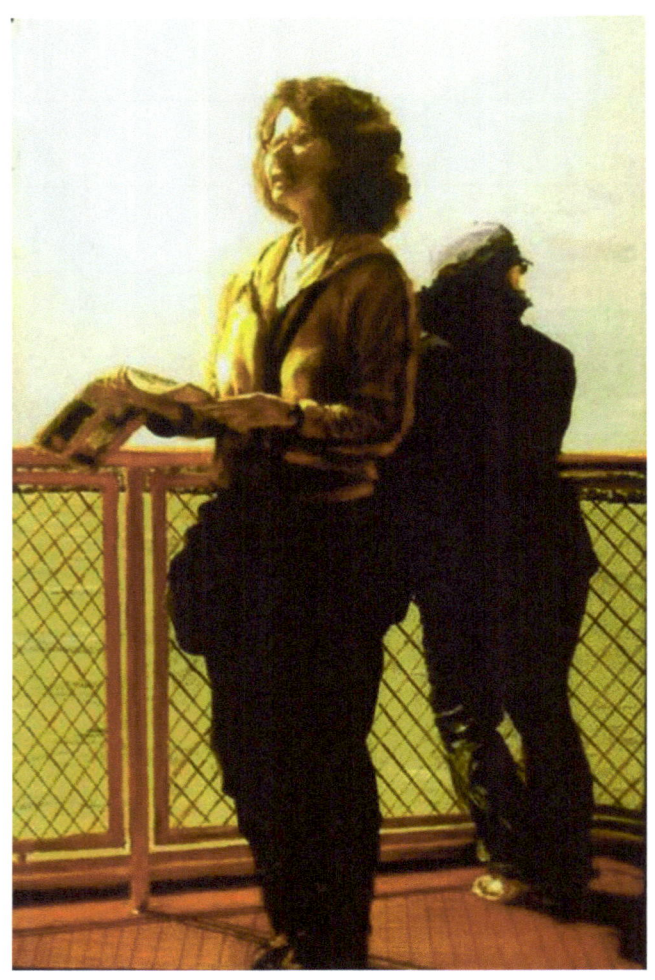

OCTOBER

Ferry takes place on the ferry from Manhattan to Staten Island. It looks at two women; one a consummate tourist and the other a typical New Yorker. But on another level they are about being engaged in life or being a casual observer. The painting is acrylic on stretched canvas on heavy duty stretchers, with painted sides. It can be seen at www.Zibbet.com/Egilpatr

OCTOBER

1 _____

2 _____

3 _____

4 _____

5 _____

6 _____

7 _____

8 _____

9 _____

10 _____

11 _____

12 _____

13 _____

14 _____

15 _____

16 _____

OCTOBER

17 _____

18 _____

19 _____

20 _____

21 _____

22 _____

23 _____

24 _____

25 _____

26 _____

27 _____

28 _____

29 _____

30 _____

31 _____

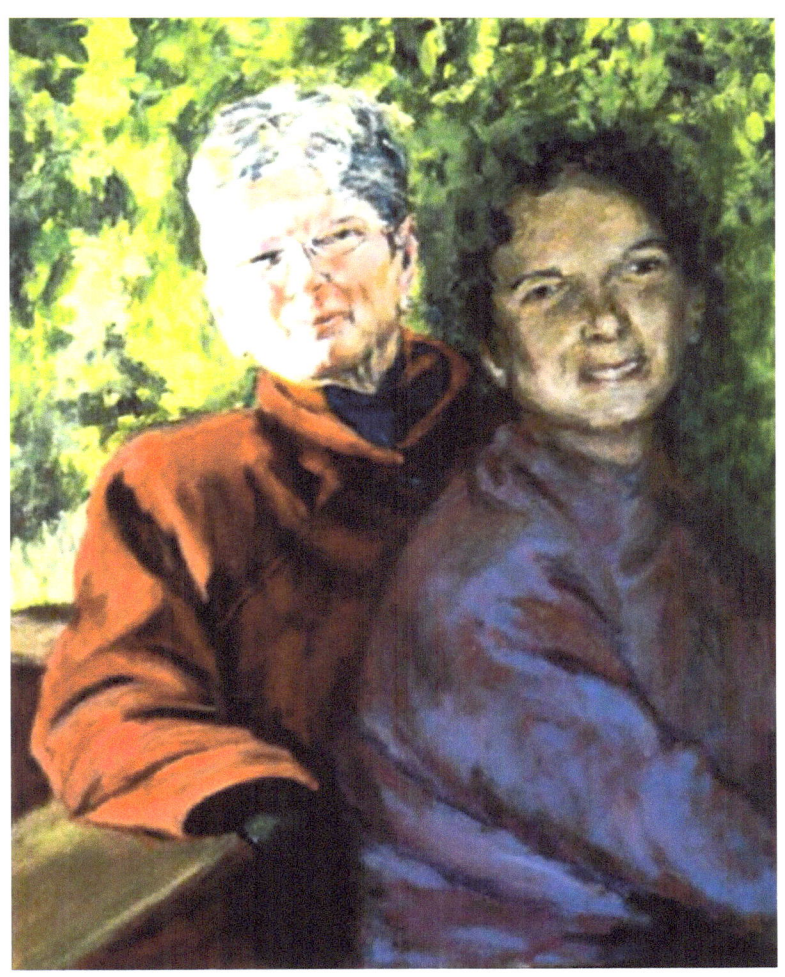

NOVEMBER

Patsy Now and Then is a double portrait of Patsy, a long lost ex-sister-in-law, shown as she was as a wedding guest many years ago, and as she was in recent years. The "remembered" image is painted with unsaturated colors, so, though it is placed forward, it fades to the background. The painting is 28 x 22 inches, acrylic, on stretched canvas, on heavy duty stretchers. The framed dimensions are 29 inches high x 23 inches wide. See it at www.Zibbet.com/Egilpatr

NOVEMBER

1 _____

2 _____

3 _____

4 _____

5 _____

6 _____

7 _____

8 _____

9 _____

10 _____

11 _____

12 _____

13 _____

14 _____

15 _____

16 _____

NOVEMBER

17 _____

18 _____

19 _____

20 _____

21 _____

22 _____

23 _____

24 _____

25 _____

26 _____

27 _____

28 _____

29 _____

30 _____

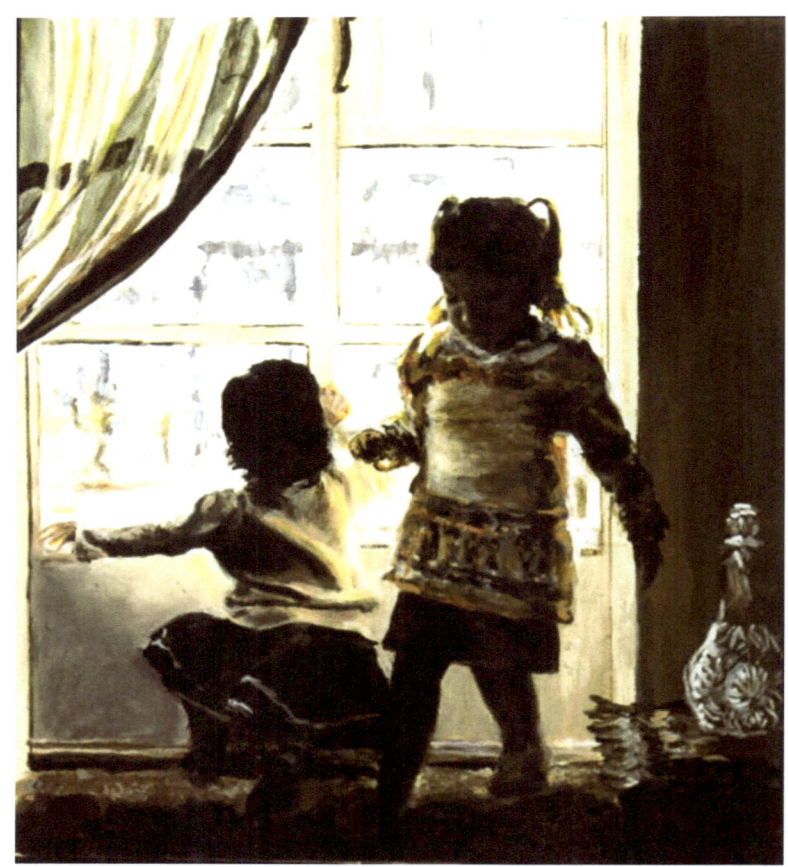

DECEMBER

Cousins is set inside my apartment. These are two of my nieces, backlit in my living room by light through the terrace doors, Christmas Eve Day, 2006. It is acrylic on canvas; the framed dimensions are 19 inches wide x 21 inches high. The painting is not for sale.

DECEMBER

1 _____

2 _____

3 _____

4 _____

5 _____

6 _____

7 _____

8 _____

9 _____

10 _____

11 _____

12 _____

13 _____

14 _____

15 _____

16 _____

DECEMBER

17 _____

18 _____

19 _____

20 _____

21 _____

22 _____

23 _____

24 _____

25 _____

26 _____

27 _____

28 _____

29 _____

30 _____

31 _____

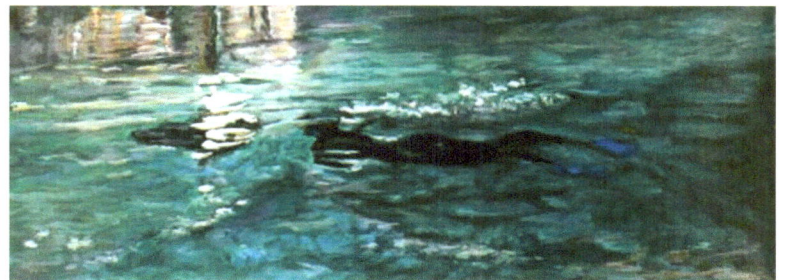

BIOGRAPHY

Eleanor Gilpatrick is a contemporary realist, painting landscapes, figural works, and still lifes that capture fragments of the world. They arrest the viewer in terms of composition, color, and content. Illustrated in this book are some of her paintings of people. These capture images of people absorbed in leading their lives; rarely are the subjects aware of being photographed.

Prior to her art career, Eleanor Gilpatrick was professor at the School of Health Sciences, Hunter College, City University of New York.

She won prizes for painting and draftsmanship in high school and at the Educational Alliance in New York City, but chose to study the social sciences in college and graduate school. She eventually became an expert in health care policy and human resources, authored four books, directed a masters program in health services administration, and pioneered courses in critical thinking and writing. She is Professor Emerita at Hunter College.

Gilpatrick picked up the thread of drawing and painting in 1998 in plein-air workshops in Italy, and returned to serious study in studio courses at Hunter College just before she retired. An inventory of her paintings is on display at:www.Zibbet.com/Egilpatr

www.ingramcontent.com/pod-product-compliance
Lightning Source LLC
Chambersburg PA
CBHW041143180526
45159CB00002BB/719